MW00913146

eat.shop kansas city

researched, photographed and written by
kaie wellman and jon hart

cabazon books : 2009

table of contents

eat

05 > **1924 main**   07 > **arthur bryant's**   09 > **babycakes**   11 > **blanc burgers + bottles**
13 > **blue grotto**   15 > **bluebird bistro**   17 > **bluestem restaurant**   19 > **broadway café & roastery**
21 > **cascone's grill**   23 > **cellar rat**   25 > **christopher elbow**   27 > **city tavern**   29 > **d'bronx**
31 > **dolce baking**   33 > **donut king**   35 > **fervere bakery**   37 > **fresher than fresh snowcones**
39 > **grinders**   41 > **habashi mart**   43 > **happy gillis**   45 > **hi hat coffee**
47 > **jerry's woodswether cafe**   49 > **jess and jim's steak house**   51 > **la cucina di mamma**
53 > **le fou frog**   55 > **lill's on 17th**   57 > **malay cafe**   59 > **mario's grinder co.**   61 > **michael smith**
63 > **murray's ice cream and cookies**   65 > **oklahoma joe's barbeque**   67 > **paleterias tropicana**
69 > **pizza bella**   71 > **po's dumpling bar**   73 > **pot pie**   75 > **room 39**   77 > **savoy grill**
79 > **songbird cafe**   81 > **stroud's**   83 > **succotash**   85 > **taqueria camecuaro**
87 > **the better cheddar**   89 > **the filling station**   91 > **the peanut**   93 > **the upper crust**
95 > **town topic**   97 > **velvet creme popcorn**   99 > **yj's snack bar**   101 > **you say tomato**

shop

119 > **45th & state line arts and antique district**   121 > **acme bicycle company**
123 > **antiquities & oddities architectural salvage**   125 > **birdies**   127 > **black bamboo**
129 > **bon bon atelier**   131 > **brookside toy & science**   133 > **creative-coldsnow**   135 > **curious sofa**
137 > **foundation**   139 > **gallup map company**   141 > **george**   143 > **habitat**   145 > **hammerpress**
147 > **harry j. epstein co.**   149 > **haught style**   151 > **hudson home**   153 > **hung-vuong market**
155 > **matney floral design**   157 > **mitzy london's**   159 > **museo**   161 > **nigro's western store**
163 > **peggy noland**   165 > **polivka**   167 > **prospero's books**   169 > **pryde's olde westport**
171 > **reading reptile**   173 > **retro inferno**   175 > **river market antique mall**   177 > **spool**
179 > **standard style**   181 > **the darling room**   183 > **the orchidloft**
185 > **the planters seed & spice company**   187 > **vinyl renaissance**   189 > **volker bikes**

kaie's + jon's notes on kc

K: I'm not big on terms like "the next big thing" or "what's hot." Usually the moment that tag is placed on something, anything, it's kind of downhill from there. So I won't make a silly statement like Kansas City is the next "it" city. What I will say is that this town is vibrant. There's a creative scene from artists and musicians to architects and designers that help give this city a strong pulse.

I have many friends that are KC natives, and now many more friends that I met while working on this book. Most of them asked Jon and me a valid question, "what took you so long to do an *eat.shop kansas city* book?" After being in the city for only a couple of hours, there was no good answer because we quickly realized that KC is a fantastic town. We had a blast from beginning to end.

A couple of things I'd like to note: the architecture is outstanding here. There's a veritable who's who of major 20th century architects who left their mark on this town. And if you have the time, take a jaunt to Lawrence, which is one of the most hoppin' college towns in the country and has a solid local eating and shopping scene.

• •

J: I was thrilled when I got my spring '09 *eat.shop* assignment. I had never visited Kansas City even though I grew up just one state away. Like Kaie, I too had many friends tell me of its incredible virtues and swear that I would love it. I was ready for an adventure and getting paid to eat barbeque sounded almost too good to be true. Full of anticipation I did a solo scouting trip in the fall of '08. It was one of those magical fall weeks that make me wistful for the midwest. The trees were turning colors and there was a crispness in the clear air. Almost immediately I met amazing, generous people who happily shared secrets about their city. Kaie called to get a report and I cut her off gushing about all the treasures I had seen.

I then checked out The Nelson-Atkins Museum, and that solidified my KC affection. It ranks high as one of the best art collections in America for good reason. The collection of de Koonings alone blew my mind. The shiny, asymmetric Kemper Museum next door will make even the most blasé of art snobs sit up and take notice.

To me Kansas City is a perfect city for both visiting and living. Its beauty and vitality are bountiful, yet the scale and population are small enough that one feels ownership and great pride. What a great town.

1924 main

cozy upscale bistro

1924 main street. corner of twentieth
816.472.1924 www.1924main.com
mon - sun 5 - close

opened in 2004. owners: rob and margarita dalzell chef: rob dalzell
$$ - $$$: all major credit cards accepted
dinner. full bar. reservations recommended

crossroads arts district >

J: Restauranteur Rob Dalzell is Kansas City's busiest dining mogul. He is the owner/chef and creator of four of the city's most loved restaurants. Is it a coincidence that one of them is named *Souperman*? I think not. At *1924 Main* the feeling is of a dapper, cozy bistro and the food is excellent. The food and the ambience are perfectly done, as they are at all of Rob's places. So you have to wonder if this guy who doesn't look much older than Jimmy Olsen has a weakness. Maybe it's kryptonite, but my guess is that the guy has a weakness for good food.

imbibe / devour:
sabio blanco cocktail
exhibition cocktail
celery root chowder
pumpkin dumplings
pork shoulder with grits
flatiron steak, mustard greens & potato purée
sea bass & twice-fried potatoes with tarragon
brownie ice cream sandwich

arthur bryant's

a kansas city institution for barbecue

1727 brooklyn avenue. corner of 18th
816.231.1123 www.arthurbryantsbbq.com
see website for other locations
mon - thu 10a - 9:30p fri - sat 10a - 10p sun 11a - 8p

opened in 1930. owners: gary berbiglia and bill rauschelbach
$$: all major credit cards accepted
lunch. dinner. first come, first served

downtown east > **e02**

J: In the world of meat, not much is argued more contentiously than what makes good barbeque. Should the sauce be sweet or vinegary? Should the meat fall off the bone, or should it have a little more tooth? There are as many arguments as answers. In Kansas City one definite answer is *Arthur Bryant's* legendary barbeque. The sauce here is complex: tart and deep, full of vinegar, with a mysterious mix of spices. The meat, smokey and tender, makes the argument that this is what the pig was born to do. Finding your favorite barbeque joint is a riveting pursuit. Just make sure *Arthur Bryant's* is on the path.

imbibe / devour:
red soda
arthur bryant's rub & sauces
burnt ends
whole slabs of ribs
pulled pork sandwich
baked beans & cole slaw
fries fried in lard
quart of pickles

babycakes

gourmet cupcakes and more

108 east missouri avenue. between grand and walnut
816.841.1048 www.babycakeskc.com
tue - fri 10a - 6p sat 10a - 4p

opened in 2006. owner: laura caron
$: all major credit cards accepted
treats. first come, first served

river market > **e03**

K: Sometimes I hit it off with the owner of a business, way before I know if I like what they are selling. This would be the case with Laura at *Babycakes*. She had Jon and me at hello. Of course it didn't hurt that this little nook of a storefront feels like cupcake heaven on earth. While listening to Laura's insightful and hysterical tales of Kansas City, Jon and I slugged down Shatto root beer milk and licked our lips at the almost-too-pretty-to-eat cupcakes and chocolates. By the time we left, we had a deep bond with Laura forged by sugar and a good dose of laughter.

imbibe / devour:
shatto milk company flavored milks
cupcakes:
   caramel with dulce de leche icing
   pumpkin with cream cheese icing
   chocolate with peanut butter icing
   lemon with lemon icing
   eggnog with vanilla icing
frou frou chocolates

blanc burgers + bottles

affordable gourmet burgers

419 westport road. between broadway and pennsylvania
816.756.3767 www.blancburgers.com
mon - thu 11a - 10p fri - sat 11a - 11p sun noon - 10p

opened in 2008. owners: ernesto peralta and jennifer price
owner / chef: josh eans
$$: all major credit cards accepted
lunch. dinner. full bar. first come, first served

westport >  e04

K: I have food anxiety dreams. One of them is that I'm served a big, meaty burger, but then I ignore it and I whip out a McDonald's cheese burger I just happen to be carrying. The scary thing is that this dream is somewhat rooted in reality. I'm often not a fan of the "gourmet burger" as they can be just too darn big with too much "stuff" loaded on. But *Blanc Burgers + Bottles* helped me get a good night's sleep. Their gourmet burgers are well-crafted but don't weigh 12 bloody pounds and have perfectly edited toppings. Plus the onion rings are a dream. Thank you *Blanc Burgers* for weaning me off of Ambien.

imbibe / devour:
dirty pickle cocktail
lost trail root beer
butter lettuce salad with green onion & fuji apple
au poivre burger
pork burger
boulevard pale ale onion rings
gin & tonic milk shakes
custard malt chocolate

11

blue grotto

wood oven pizzas

6324 brookside plaza. between 63rd and meyer
816.361.3473 www.bluegrottobrookside.com
mon - sat 11a - 1:30a sun 4p - 2a

opened in 2008. owner: john grier owner / chef: chris graham
$ - $$: mc. visa
lunch. dinner. full bar. reservations accepted for parties of eight or more

brookside >

J: Did you know that of the three billion or so pizzas consumed in the United States each year, almost two billion of those are pepperoni? And of those, over 99% taste more or less exactly the same. You know what I mean: cardboard crust, sweet bland sauce, only good when you are drunk. Thankfully there's hope in the remaining 1% which includes *Blue Grotto's* handmade, wood-fired delicacies. Made with top-notch ingredients like housemade fennel sausage, crimini mushrooms and fresh leeks, *Blue Grotto* is one in a million.

imbibe / devour:
boulevard pale ale
king estate pinot noir
grotto azurra salad
italian hard salami sandwich
salsiccia pizza
porri pizza
blackberry cream cheese ice cream &
  pound cake terrine

blue bird bistro

organic neighborhood bistro
1700 summit. corner of 17th
816.221.7559 www.kansascitymenus.com/bluebirdbistro
mon - sat 7a - 10p sun 10a - 2p

opened in 2001. owner: jane zieha chef: lisa yamanaka
$$: mc. visa
breakfast. lunch. dinner. full bar. reservations recommended

westside north > e06

J: I'm a bistroholic. I will fess up to this addiction with no shame, no regret. When I go to a new city I scour the neighborhoods looking for that hit of warm and comfortable, buzzy and charming—my definition of a good bistro. In Kansas City, *Blue Bird Bistro* fits my bill. With its mosaic tile floor and pressed tin ceiling, its charm was delightful. As for the food: I started to get the shakes as I waited for my killer tomato sandwich I was so excited. One bite and I was in sweet bliss. I don't think there is anything wrong with my addiction as long as bistros like *Blue Bird* are my drug of choice.

imbibe / devour:
maple leaf martini
domaine les palliers gigondas
killer tomato sandwich
blue bird benedict
bison burger
stuffed squash with curried quinoa
double cut pork chop with apple chutney
apple crostata with chantilly cream

15

bluestem restaurant

progressive american cuisine

900 westport road. corner of 58th court
816.561.1101 www.bluestemkc.com
tue - sat 5 - 11p sun 10:30a - 2:30p

opened in 2004. owner / chefs: colby and megan garrelts
$$ - $$$: all major credit cards accepted
brunch. dinner. reservations recommended

westport >

K: I am a hypocrite. I complain often about how spoiled we've become when it comes to dining, and how people should accept, as is, what a chef offers. But then I'm the first to ask for something on the side. Silly me. Options really are a good thing when it comes to dining, and at *Bluestem* there are some neat ones. You can choose among a three-, five-, seven- or twelve-course meal or opt for a la carte (and don't forget about gorgeous brunch). Neato. And what's even neater are the prices. For this quality of cuisine and for that matter quantity, you're getting a deal. So no complaining, okay?

imbibe / devour:
the emerald city
missouri pears, maytag, beets & arugula
wagyu tartare, black olive caramel & potato crisps
pumpkin gnocchi, spiced squash & sage
roasted halibut with lemon parsley orzo
campo lindo hen with prosciutto & hominy
bittersweet chocolate pudding cake
snacks & small plates in the bar

broadway café & roastery

local coffee roaster

café: 4106 broadway. between westport and archibald
roastery: 4012 washington. near 40th
816.531.2432 www.broadwaycafeandroastery.com
c: daily 7a - 9p / r: mon - fri 7a - 6p sat 8a - 6p sun 8a - 5p

opened in 1992. owners: jon cates and sara honan
$: all major credit cards accepted
coffee / tea. treats. first come, first served

westport > e08

J: When I grew up in the Midwest, getting an espresso meant driving thirty or so miles to a Chicago suburb. My friends and I used to think we were so cool making that trip for our exotic caffeine fix. That was a long time ago, and now (scarily enough) you can get a latte with your Big Mac. But, *Broadway Café & Roastery* compels you to go the extra mile. Here they roast their own beans and really know what is involved in making a velvety and smooth, rich and satisfying coffee drink. Yes, the times have changed, but quality is still worth the trip.

imbibe / devour:
perfectly pulled espresso drinks made from
house-roasted beans:
  espresso
  cappuccino
  mocha
  macchiato
frosted "soft" scone
chocolate layer cake

cascone's grill

old-school lunch counter
17 east fifth street. between grand and delaware
816.471.1018
tue - sat 6a - 2p

opened in 1930. owners: the cascone family
$: all major credit cards accepted
breakfast. lunch. first come, first served

river market > **e09**

J: *Cascone's Grill* is an old-school breakfast and lunch spot untouched by time. But it is a time of which I am very fond. They do not serve espresso but steaming mugs of drip coffee, margarine is in its heydey still, and talk of dieting is unheard of which is fortunate because at *Cascone's* nothing seems more appropriate after a big plate of meatloaf and gravy or the unapologetically addictive "Big Sam" than a healthy slice of coconut cream pie. I love that great lunch counters like this still exist. A classic never goes out of style.

imbibe / devour:
hot chocolate
good old drip coffee
pig hock & beans
tips & noodles
"the big sam" sandwich
baked meatloaf with gravy
bowl of custard
coconut cream pie

cellar rat

wine merchants and more

1701 baltimore avenue. corner of 17th
816.224.9463 www.cellarratwine.com
mon - sat 10a - 9p

opened in 2006. owners: john opelka and ryan sciara
$$: all major credit cards accepted
wine / beer. first come, first served

crossroads arts district > e10

J: I like having these things: good friends, conversation and laughs. There are a couple of ways to have these consistently: befriend David Sedaris and have him over all of the time or keep your same friends and include wine in the mix. And, to keep them happy, it better be good wine. This means going to a store that knows the difference between a Pinot Noir and pee in a jar. *Cellar Rat* does. Their selection is outstanding and their assistance helpful. Participating in some of their frequent tastings and classes is a good way to hone your wine language. Helpful stuff as your circle of friends grows.

imbibe / devour:
cakebread cabernet sauvignon
lange pinot noir
loring wine company
remarkable vanilla porter
tentaka kuni junmai sake
cheeses!
patric chocolates
wine classes & club

christopher elbow

artisanal chocolates

1819 mcgee street. between 18th and 19th
816.842.1300 www.elbowchocolates.com
tue - sat 10a - 6p

opened in 2003. owner: christopher elbow
$ - $$: all major credit cards accepted
treats. first come, first served

crossroads arts district > **e11**

K: Mr. Elbow, meet Ms. Hand. Ms. Hand will be reaching out to lovingly cradle one of your rosemary caramel chocolates and then transfer it to the neighboring mouth. Okay, I'll stop with this nonsense as *Christopher Elbow's* chocolates are seriously good. Good on the level that few tread. So good that you want to empty your bank account buying forty-two piece collections for everybody you know and complete strangers you meet on the street. So good that you write a guide about local eating and shopping in KC and try to figure out how to subliminally mention these chocolates throughout the book.

imbibe / devour:
drinking chocolate
chocolates:
 rosemary caramel
 russian tea
 banana curry
 fresh lime
 cinnamon with candied pecan
fleur de sel turtles

city tavern

stylish tavern in the historic freight house

101 west 22nd street. end of baltimore
816.421.3696 www.citytavern.net
lunch mon - fri 11a - 2p dinner mon - thu 5 - 9p fri - sat 5 - 10p

opened in 2002. owner: dan clothier chef: jason czaja
$$ - $$$: all major credit cards accepted
lunch. dinner. reservations recommended

crossroads arts district > **e12**

K: On the last night Jon and I were working on this book, we met up with our pals Brady and Lindsay at *City Tavern*. We were wacky tired as we always are after intensive eating and shopping (right, I hear the violins too). Brady and Lindsay were fried too, so we all were sub-human puddles propped up on stools. Then *City Tavern* worked its magic on us. A drink or two (okay three) later and some good food and we were revived... so revived that we could have happily eaten through the whole menu. So revived, we shut the place down. *City Tavern* is a panacea—I highly recommend a dose.

imbibe / devour:
moscow mule
blanton's small batch bourbon
iced seafood platter
midwestern charcuterie
baby iceberg wedge salad
shellfish pot pie
city tavern bouillabaisse
kansas city beef duo

d' bronx

authentic deli and pizzeria

3904 bell street. corner of 39th
816.531.0550 www.dbronxkc.com (see website for other locations)
mon - thu 10:30a - 9p fri - sat 10:30a - 11p sun noon - 8p

opened in 1990. owners: don forienger
$ - $$: all major credit cards accepted
lunch. dinner. first come, first served

westport >

K: Sometimes when working on these books I don't eat all day, where every place I go to is focused on the shop side of this book. I had one of these days in KC, while Jon had the exact opposite experience, eating something like eight meals So when our day ended together at *D'Bronx*, I wasn't sharing a thing with Mr. Mealhog. I ordered the special sub and d-e-v-o-u-r-e-d it like a lion in the wild after six months of drought and one small beast crossing its path. Boom! Food gone. Of course, you don't have to be a ravenous beast to devour the food here. Everything is good and hits just the right spot.

imbibe / devour:
fresh limeade
big ole coke
shrimp bisque
olive salad
d'bronx special sub
handcrafted pizzas
baked lasagna dinner
d'bronx cheesecake

dolce baking

delicious baked goods

6974 mission road. in the prairie village shopping center
913.236.4411 www.dolcebakingco.com
tue - fri 7a - 5p sat - sun 8a - 2p

opened in 2007. owner / chef: erin reynolds
$: mc. visa
treats. coffee / tea. first come, first served

prairie village > **e14**

J: Sure it's thoughtful to make someone a home-made birthday cake—it's all about the gesture right? But I would argue, who wants a lopsided, dry cake to celebrate a day that is already sort of depressing (for anybody over 29)? Instead, I would suggest getting a delicious delicacy from *Dolce Baking*. Erin specializes in baked goods of the home style, blue ribbon variety. Her winning treats will not only make your friends and loved ones happy, but they will benefit you as well, right? After all, who can say no to a slice of something as divine as a *Dolce* cake?

imbibe / devour:
broadway roasting coffee
pecan sticky roll
dolce granola
bittersweet chocolate mousse tart
pumpkin cheesecake with ginger snap crust
sweet potato scones with maple glaze
caramel apple tarts
custom cakes

donut king

the name says it all

3913 north chouteau trafficway. between parvin and russell
816.452.2012
mon - sun 5a - 9p

opened in 1969. owners: john and lauren cone
$: mc. visa
treats. first come, first served

outer kansas city (ks) > **e15**

K: Why do I crave donuts? It's a bit of a nonsensical fixation on my part. I get the donut itch, then I go to scratch it and invariably halfway through the donut I feel disappointed and don't eat the rest. Either it's too doughy, too oily, too something. Yet I still go town to town searching for the perfect donut to bring me joy. Hence, Jon and I arrived at the somewhat out-of-the-way *Donut King*. Jon doesn't have the same feelings for donuts that I do, so he wasn't quivering with anticipation like me. So was I foiled again? All I can say is that the glazed long john was fried dough satisfaction.

imbibe / devour:
donuts with fillings:
  strawberry
  raspberry
  lemon
  cream
glazed long johns with filling
caramel pecan cinnamon rolls
apple fritters

fervere bakery

hearth-baked breads

1702 summit. corner of 17th
816.842.7272
thu - fri 11a - sellout sat 9:30a - 2p
(note: get here early for best selection)

opened in 2000. owner / baker: fred spompinato
$: cash
bakery. first come, first served

westside north > **e16**

J: Fred, the owner of *Fervere Bakery*, told me that the most important part of his small bakery was the hand-built wood-burning brick oven. Initially I believed him. The oven is impressive, occupying the entire back of the small space. But, as Fred explained his baking process, I began to suspect he was not telling me the whole truth. He noted that he mixes the dough in the afternoon and then stays up all night shaping, proofing and baking each loaf. I realized that though the oven is important, what really makes *Fervere's* brilliant loaves sing is Fred and his passion for the craft.

imbibe / devour:
breads:
   pain complet
   ciabatta
   orchard
   olive rosemary
   pain de campagne
   polenta
   cheese slippers

fresher than fresh snowcones

gourmet snowcones

address varies (check website for dates, locations and hours)
fresherthanfreshsnowcones.blogspot.com

opened in 2008. owner: lindsay laricks
$: cash
treats. first come, first served

all over town > e17

J: Rule one of business is give the people what they want. Rule two is make sure your business is unique. The lovely Lindsay obviously did well in her business classes because she opened one of the smartest enterprises I have come across is some time. *Fresher Than Fresh* snowcones is a trailer that she parks outside of various events to sell her signature snowcones. There are no strange artificial flavors used, just natural, gourmet flavors concocted by her to make your mouth water and your willpower weak. *Fresher Than Fresh* is smarter than smart.

imbibe / devour:
snowcones:
  daredevil special
  lemon prickly pear
  blackberry lavender
  espresso with mexican cane sugar
  ginger rose
  green tea pear
  watermelon basil

grinders

grinders, pizza, beer and so much more

417 east eighteenth street. corner of locust
816.472.5454 www.grinderspizza.com
mon - sun 11a - 1:30a

opened in 2004. owners: anton kotar and stretch
$ - $$: mc. visa
lunch. dinner. full bar. first come, first served

crossroads arts district > **e18**

J: *Grinders* is not simply a restaurant selling meatballs on bread. It's its own universe. Anton and Stretch started this enterprise almost by accident while drinking some brews and sharing their love of East Coast classic foods like Philly cheesesteaks. Their casual conversation turned into an institution. Events like concerts in the huge back yard to having George the Hungarian Night on Mondays (don't ask, just go) are legendary. The menu, which includes pizza with chili and tater tots may be as unconventional as the business plan, but both are a huge success.

imbibe / devour:
boulevard double wide ipa
hitachino nest sweet stout
famous chili bomb pizza with tots, chili,
    cheese & scallions
bengal tiger pizza
meatball & sausage grinders
south philly cheesesteak
the double wide

habashi mart

mediterranean and middle eastern groceries

313 main street. in the river market
816.421.6727 www.habishihouse.com
mon - fri 9a - 6p sat 7a - 5p sun 9a - 5p

opened in 1991. owners: hashem abuaisheh and ahmad habashi
$: mc. visa
grocery. first come, first served

river market >  e19

J: I'm a big fan of food packaging. It's more enjoyable to buy something that comes in an intriguingly designed box than in some generic container. That said, I am unwilling to pay ten bucks for a can of *Dean and Deluca* cumin. Instead, I buy my herbs, spices and dried goods in bulk. At *Habishi Mart*, not only are all of the above incredibly affordable, they are displayed in large open barrels to see, smell and be inspired by. Purchasing a fresh, inexpensive bag of fragrant coriander seeds can transport you to Turkey rather than make you feel like one.

imbibe / devour:
brood malt honey drink
vimto soda
green coffee beans
puck cream cheese spread
iranian watermelon seeds
bulk spices
oblatine vafel
dried lemons

happy gillis

café and hangout

549 gillis street. corner of pacific
816.471.3663 www.happysoupeater.com
tue - fri 8a - 6:30p sat 8a - 5p sun 9a - 2p

opened in 2008. owner / chef: todd schulte
$ - $$: mc. visa
breakfast. lunch. wine / beer only. first come, first served

columbus park > **e20**

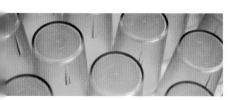

J: Todd is clearly a happy person, and he likes to spread the joy. The proof: He first opened a business called *The Happy Soupeater* where he home-delivered his freshly made soups. That's nice. Then he opened *Happy Gillis*, a café and all-around neighborhood hangout. Here he expands on his soup menu, adding exemplary sandwiches like a croque madame and the classic vietnamese bahn mi sandwich. It's all so good, what could make you happier? A big savings account and a vacation somewhere maybe? Devoid of these options, try a yummy brownie—it's happiness guaranteed.

imbibe / devour:
fizzy lizzy drinks
new belgium abby ale
croque madame
not my mom's meatloaf
bahn mi sandwich
housemade granola & yogurt
fresh bialys
yummy brownies

43

hi hat coffee

biggest little coffee shop in the country

5012 state line. corner of 50th
913.722.5000 www.hihatcoffee.com
mon - fri 7a - 5:30p sat 8a - 5:30p

opened in 1999. owner: t. jensen
$: all major credit cards accepted
coffee / tea. treats. first come, first served

inner kansas city (ks) > e21

K: I think in a previous life I was a munchkin because I like little places. Two-hundred-seat restaurants give me the heebie-jeebies, but twenty-seat-places feel just right. Concerts with thousands of people are annoying, but tiny clubs are blissful. Coffeehouses where there are rows of people feverishly tap-tap-tapping away on their laptop keyboards while slurping coffee is not my cup of tea, and yet the miniscule *Hi Hat Coffee* is perfection. With enough room inside for a couple of people to stand and a couple more to sit, it's coziness personified and the coffee is good. Here's to the little places!

imbibe / devour:
jet tea
iced cherry flip
coffees:
   black & white
   avalanche
   nutty irishman
palmiers
bam bam

jerry's woodswether cafe

hearty spot for hardy types

1414 ninth street. between hickory and liberty
816.472.6333
mon - fri 5:30a - 3p sat 6a - 1p

owner: jerry naster
$: all major credit cards accepted
breakfast. lunch. first come, first served

west bottoms > **e22**

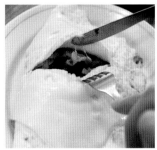

K: I could go on and on about the amazing architectural landscape of KC, but for this blurb I'll just yap about West Bottoms, where *Jerry's Woodswether Cafe* is located. It's a ghostown of dilapidated red brick warehouses that are photographically enigmatic. Areas like this across urban America have been glossed up and loftified, and maybe this will happen here—but for now imagine what it was back in the day of the KC Stock Exchange and hang with the locals at *Jerry's*. There's nothing swank about *Jerry's* and that's a good thing, especially when it comes to big ole breakfasts and mountainous lunches.

imbibe / devour:
shakes & malts
ice tea
popeye omelette & grits
the big john
catfish fridays (fried frog legs too!)
patty melts, reubens & big old cheeseburgers
chicken fried steak
deep-fried brownie

47

jess and jim's steak house

classic kansas city steakhouse

517 east 135th street. between locust and holmes
816.941.9499 www.jessandjims.com
mon - sat 11a - 10p sun noon - 9p

opened in 1938. owners: mike and david van noy
$$ - $$$: mc. visa
lunch. dinner. full bar. first come, first served

martin city >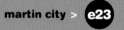

K: My grandparents raised Herefords, and some of my best memories of being at their farm are of hanging out with the cows, scratching their backs, hand-feeding them hay. My brother and I were most fond of Blackie. Then one day Blackie disappeared and re-appeared in our freezer. Vegetarianism ensued. That is, until I smelled a steak cooking the next week. I then forever accepted that I was a carnivore. Hence, I love *Jess and Jim's*. This place is the real deal. There's no flash here. All of the fireworks go into sourcing the best meat and then preparing it well. Viva the cow!

imbibe / devour:
bombay martini
maker's mark manhattan
fried asparagus
angus filet
kc strip
beef tips & noodles
prime rib
incredibly huge baked potatoes

49

la cucina di mamma

delicious homestyle italian café connected to bella napoli

6227 brookside boulevard. between 62nd and 63rd
816.444.1138 www.kcbellanapoli.com
mon - thu 11a - 8p fri - sat 11a - 9p

opened in 2006. owner / chef: jake imperiale
$ - $$: mc. visa
lunch. dinner. wine / beer. grocery. first come, first served

brookside >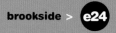

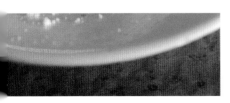

J: I have heard people say that it's hard to get a bad meal in Italy. My experience leads me to concur. Even a small Italian café serving the simplest of foods can be extraordinary. My meal at *La Cucina di Mamma* made me think I was at one of those amazing little places. The food here is simple. Rigatoni with meat sauce, sautéed spinach with butter and parmesan—all made by caring, knowledgeable hands and with high quality ingredients. And what makes it better is that it's a part of a great market, *Bella Napoli*, where the best Italian ingredients can come home with you to roost in your kitchen.

imbibe / devour:
house red wine
pizza pugliese
rigatoni with meat sauce
housemade gnocchi with tomato & basil
melanzanie parmigiana
scaloppini di vitello
sautéed spinach with butter & parmesan
homemade cream puffs

51

le fou frog

a delightul french bistro

400 east fifth street. corner of oak
816.474.6060 www.lefoufrog.com
tue - thu 4:30 - 10p fri - sat 5 - 11p sun 5 - 9p

opened in 1996. owner / chef: osmane rafael owner: barbara rafael
$$ - $$$: all major credit cards accepted
lunch. dinner. happy hour. full bar. reservations recommended

river market > **e25**

K: I keep handy a list of words that I like. For some reason I'm especially fond of terms like knick-knacks, thingamajigs and doohickeys. *Le Fou Frog* is filled to the brim with all three which makes for a charming little spot that feels a bit like you're dining in your French grandmere's sitting room. Mano has a whimsical touch with the food that matches the décor, and it is my suggestion that you relax and be swept away by the romance of it all. Put away all crazy-making communication devices and cradle in your hand an aperitif instead.

imbibe / devour:
pierre chermette beaujolais villages
lillet blanc
assiette de caviar domestique
tartare de thon
le rouget rose avec de coulis
lobster tails, vanilla beans & champagne
pheasant, benedictine & truffles
gateau au chocolat avec caramel & fleur de sel

lill's on 17th

adorable neighborhood café

815 west 17th street. between summit and madison
816.421.4441 www.kansascitymenus.com/lillson17th
wed - thu 11a - 2p 5 - 9p fri - sat 11a - 2p 5:30 - 10p

opened in 2005. owner: trelle osteen chefs: ken fletcher and david allison
$$: all major credit cards accepted
lunch. dinner. reservations recommended

westside north > **e26**

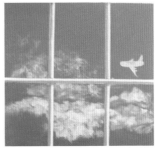

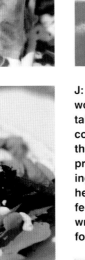

J: It makes sense to me that a former flight attendant would make a good restaurant owner. If you have a talent at taking care of people and making them feel comfortable, what is so different about doing it in the air or on the ground? The owner of *Lill's on 17th* proves that there is no difference. After a life of asking the question, "Chicken or beef," Trelle opened her own place. How liberating it must be to finally feel good about the fare you are offering like bacon-wrapped dates and peach bread pudding. This is food you would kill for on a trans-atlantic flight.

imbibe / devour:
trumpeter malbec
raimat cabernet sauvignon
mussels with white wine & aromatics
bacon wrapped dates
crab cakes with homemade remoulade
atlantic salmon salad with cilantro lime aioli
sautéed shrimp with butter & garlic
peach bread pudding

malay cafe

classic malaysian cuisine

6003 northwest barry road. between st. clair and barrybrook
816.741.3616
mon - thu 11a - 9:30p fri - sat 11a - 10p

opened in 2001. owner / chef: bill fang
$ - $$: mc. visa
lunch. dinner. wine / beer. first come, first served

north kansas city > **e27**

K: I must throw out a disclaimer about *Malay Cafe*—it's a bit out of the way unless you happen to be going to the airport, leaving the airport or living in the surrounding area. Disclaimer aside, I will suggest that even if you are in downtown KC in the middle of the day, a drive to *Malay Cafe* will be well worth your while. Why? First, there's no other place in town serving the foods of Malaysia. Second, Malaysian cuisine is utterly delicious and distinctly different from Thai and other Asian cuisines with its use of lemongrass, keffir limes, pandan, etc. Trust me—you'll be hooked at first bite.

imbibe / devour:
malaysia kopi
tarik
satay
gado gado
nasi goreng
laksa lemak
bob chacha
malay parfait

57

mario's grinder co.

classic grinders

204 westport road. between wyandotte and central
816.531.7187 www.marioswestport.com
mon - sat 11a - 3p

opened in 1976. owner: john waid
$: all major credit cards accepted
lunch. first come, first served

westport >

J: After placing my lunch order at *Mario's*, the waiter noted, "That is the perfect lunch." Feeling pleased with myself, I sat back and waited. I looked around the tiny dining room to see that nearly everyone else was eating the same combo. Had they all been coerced into ordering the same thing? If not, why had no one wavered from the simple combo? The answer came soon enough in the form of a perfect sausage grinder: a crispy, hollowed-out roll filled with spicy sausage and on the side, the signature pasta salad. It may not have been revolutionary, but it was exactly what I wanted—the perfect lunch indeed.

imbibe / devour:
fresh-made lemonade
grinders:
  meatball
  sausage
  cheese
  chicken
hot ham & salami
canoli

michael smith

modern american cuisine

1900 main. corner of 19th
816.842.2202 www.michaelsmithkc.com
lunch tue - fri 11:30a - 2p dinner tue - sat 5 - 10p

opened in 2007. owner / chef: michael smith owner: nancy smith
$$ - $$$: all major credit cards accepted
lunch. dinner. reservations recommended

crossroads arts district > e29

K: I may be showing a lack of verbal maturity by describing *Michael Smith* (the restaurant) with just one word: yum. I could see where you might want a bit more from me, so I'll give you this: really yummy. When I'm shooting, I try not to lick the plate, but I think Michael (the person) caught me sopping up the last fragments of the duck ragu. Yum. And the tart listed below? There's really no word to describe how good it was except… yum. And I would be remiss if i didn't tell you about Extra Virgin next door which was not yet open at press time. I assure you, it will be… yum.

imbibe / devour:
francois montand sparkling wine
campo lindo chicken livers
tuscan duck ragu
smith burger & pommes frites
sauteed pacific swordfish
roasted p.e.i. mussels
chocolate cherry tart
pasilla chile chocolate cake

murray's ice creams & cookies

beloved ice cream shop
4210 pennsylvania avenue. corner of 42nd
816.931.5646
wed - thu 10a - 10:30p fri - sun 10a - 11p (closed december - march)

opened in 1984. owner: murray
$: mc. visa
treats. first come, first served

westport >

K: When I'm working on these books, I read Chowhound, following hundreds of threads in reference to food establishments in a city. Usually the conversation is the back and forth about who likes this or dislikes that, but I've never seen a discussion about when an ice cream shop was going to re-open after its traditional winter break. This was the case with *Murray's*. Opening day here must be like the opening day of baseball. I wonder if there's a parade? I would happily be first in line to get just about anything on their big ole menu, including any of their tongue-in-cheek-named ice creams.

imbibe / devour:
new york egg cremes
brown cows & black cows
murraycano (americano)
malt licka ice cream
one drunk monk ice cream
sundaes! (cookie monster sundae)
banana splits
anything with blue goo

MURRAY'S
est. 1984

oklahoma joe's barbeque

rockin' good bbq

3002 west 47th avenue. corner of mission
913.722.3366 www.oklahomajoesbbq.com
mon - thu 11a - 8:30p fri - sat 11a - 9:30p

opened in 1996. owner: jeff stehney
$ - $$: all major credit cards accepted
lunch. dinner. first come, first served

inner kansas city (ks) >

K: The last time I waited in line at a gas station was in '74, rolling around the back of my mom's wood-paneled station wagon. That was until I went to *Oklahoma Joe's*. Yes, it's a barbeque joint masquerading as a gas station convenience store. Original concept I must say. Though you might be afraid that the food is along the lines of greasy jo-jo's and jalapeño corn nuts, this is some of the best barbeque in Kansas City. Many argue it *is* the best, outgunning the classics—*Arthur Bryant's* and *Gates*. I'm not going to weigh in on this discussion except to say that the bbq here is smokin' good.

imbibe / devour:
beer
smoked chicken gumbo
pulled pork sandwich
the hog heaven sandwich
pit boss salad
smoked chicken dinner
ribs & one meat dinner
good fries

paleterias tropicana

estilo michoacan

830 southwest boulevard. near summit
816.221.0192 www.paleteriastropicana.com
(see website for other locations)
daily 8a - 11p

opened in 2004. owner: jose luis valdez
$: all major credit cards accepted
treats. first come, first served

west side > **e32**

K: Every night my daughter makes a beeline for the freezer whether it be in the heat of summer or the freeze of winter. She roots around, always searching for one of her beloved popsicles. She's especially fond of the Mexican popsicles (paletas) that are like rice pudding on a stick. One day we couldn't find them anymore. Tragedy. Thank goodness for *Paleterias Tropicana*. Not only do they have arroz paletas, but a veritable smorgasbord of other flavors. And beyond the 'sicles, there's an amazing treat selection here, like the world's most delicious fruit salad spiked with cayenne.

imbibe / devour:
jugos naturales
cocktel de frutas naturales
paletas:
  pepino (cucumber & chili)
  arroz
escamochas
elotes
churros

pizza bella

wood-fired pizza

1810 baltimore. between 18th and 19th
816.421.7492 www.pizzabellakc.com
mon - sat 11a - 10p sun noon - 9p

opened in 2007. owner: rob dalzell chef: spencer whitaker
$$: all major credit cards accepted
lunch. dinner. first come, first served

crossroads arts district >

K: Many people talk about taking a break from meat or cutting glutens and white sugar from their diet, but have you ever heard of somebody who has decided to give up pizza? Don't lie. You haven't. Nobody gives up pizza. The reason why? Because the human body over time has morphed into a vessel that requires pizza to survive (read it in the New England Journal of Medicine). I therefore suggest numerous visits to *Pizza Bella*, where nutritious wood-fired, chewy-crusted, pizza pies await you. There's a topping for every taste bud. Oh, and make sure to wash it down with a healthy dose of chianti.

imbibe / devour:
a good chianti
peroni
trio of olive oils
prosciutto pizza
biancoverde pizza
lamb shank with white beans
brussels sprouts with pancetta vinaigrette
dolce de leche gelato

po's dumpling bar

cantonese delights

1715 west 39th street. between bell and genessee
816.931.5991 www.posdumplingandnoodle.com
lunch mon - fri 11a - 4p dinner daily until 9p

opened in 2006. owner: po hwang owner / chef: rita hwang
$ - $$: all major credit cards accepted
lunch. dinner. full bar. first come, first served

39th >

K: There are certain foods that I find restorative: my husband's roast chicken. My mother's scrambled eggs. My daughter's chocolate chip cookies. And now Rita's pork with cabbage soup. On a cold day that felt like it would never end, Jon and I headed to *Po's Dumpling Bar* in hopes that it would revive us. It did. Yes the dumplings were delicious, but the soup made me feel good from head to toe, and there was enough to feed both of us and our neighboring diners. And if for some reason we weren't satisfied, Rita was there watching us like a mother hen—vigilant about our satisfaction. We felt loved.

imbibe / devour:
the concubine special
red apple bubble tea
emperor's dumplings
cha su buns
pork with cabbage soup
mussels in black bean sauce
mother o's pork over rice
steamed sponge

pot pie

comforting food in a comforting space

904 westport road. between madison and roanoke
816.561.2702 www.kcpotpie.com
tue - thu 11a - 10p fri 11a - 11p sat 5 - 11p

opened in 2003. owner / chef: john williams owner: sarah williams
$ - $$: all major credit cards accepted
lunch. dinner. wine / beer. reservations recommended

westport > **e35**

J: What is more comforting than a chicken pot pie? A soft blanky? Grandma's embrace? It's hard to say because it's hard to beat the combination of meat, vegetables, gravy and tender crust that combined are pure heaven. And so is *Pot Pie*. It's a neighborhood place in the best sense: cozy atmosphere, well-made but unfussy food, and a wine and cocktail list that makes you glad you live in the environs. The chalkboard menu changes daily and features classics like strip steak with fries and pan-roasted chicken. But don't worry. If you are feeling a little needy, the eponymous dish is always available.

imbibe / devour:
groth sauvignon blanc
chapoutier belleruche cotes du rhône
beef and mushroom pot pie
pan-roasted chicken
strip steak with steak fries
butter lettuce salad with lemon shallot dressing
grilled cheese with soup or salad
berry cobbler with homemade ice cream

room 39

seasonal american food

1719 west 39th street. between bell and genessee
816.753.3939 www.rm39.com
see website for second location and hours

opened in 2004. owner / chefs: ted habiger and andy sloan
$$ - $$$: all major credit cards accepted
breakfast. lunch. dinner. full bar. reservations recommended

39th >

K: Even though Burger King has dominance over the term, "have it your way," I think that *Room 39* does a better job at the whole have-it-your-way deal. Feeling like breakfast? Go to *Room 39*. Hankering for lunch or dinner? *Room 39*. Live in midtown or up north? *Room 39*. See what I mean? I think ye olde Burger King best back off from that phrase. Not only does this place make things convenient for the diner, they make delish food rooted in comfort. Not so much in the meatloaf sense, but more in the modern american food vernacular of porcini-rubbed ribeye. Catch me—I'm swooning.

imbibe / devour:
the outsider
fernet branca & ginger ale
oven eggs
porcini gnocchi
borlotti & northern bean soup with turnip greens
porcini-dusted sweetbreads
braised berkshire pork shank
sherry pound cake with chestnut ice cream

savoy grill

gracious dining at an old-school legend

219 west ninth street. corner of central
816.842.3890 www.savoygrill.net
mon - thu 11a - 11p fri - sat 11a - 11:30p sun 4 - 10p

opened in 1903. chef: t.j. stack
$$ - $$$: all major credit cards accepted
lunch. dinner. full bar. reservations recommended

downtown >

K: Though I love to eat at "new" restaurants, my favorites are ones that have been "around the block" in a manner of speaking. Places where the wood is old and often the servers are older. Where gimlets are still de rigueur and dishes like sole meuniere are favorites. Restaurants that fall into this category are *Tadich Grill* in San Francisco, *Musso & Frank's* in Hollywood and the *Savoy Grill* in KC. Walking in here feels like entering the Emerald City—everything gleams with a deep patina. Couples tucked into the deep booths were savoring martinis and lobster. This is how restaurants were meant to be.

imbibe / devour:
louis roederer cristal
barnett pinot noir
coquilles saint jacques
shrimp de jonghe
whole maine lobster
chateau briand for two
tournedos rossini
rhum baba flambé

songbird cafe

the cutest little cafe in the middle of nowhere
1315 fairfax trafficway. across from the grain elevators
www.songbirdcafe.blogspot.com
mon - fri 7a - 3p (ish)

opened in 2008. owner / chef: courtney wasson
$: mc. visa
breakfast. lunch. early dinner. first come, first served

fairfax district >

K: Where do you imagine toughies like truckers and dudes who climb up poles and wrangle power lines go to eat? Greasy dives that serve chipped beef on toast come to mind. Imagine the exact opposite—the *Songbird Cafe*. Located across from whopping big grain elevators, this little sliver of a place is light-filled, smells like warm bread and is decorated in festive pastels. On the stove is a pan of soup and two ol' toughies are digging into their bowls and grilled sandwiches while eyeing the baked goods on the counter. This is what I like about this town. It's not always what you'll think it will be.

imbibe / devour:
fresh coffee
french toast casserole
courtney's chili & cornbread
salami & swiss melt
grilled cheese & tomato soup
oatmeal chocolate cranberry cookie
cherry crisp
whatever's cooking on courtney's stove

stroud's

the home of pan-fried chicken

north: 5410 northeast oak ridge drive. across from timber ridge golf course
south: 4200 shawnee mission parkway. near 55th
n: 816.454.9600 / s: 913.262.8500 www.stroudsrestaurant.com
see website for hours

opened in 1933. owner: mike donegan
$$: all major credit cards accepted
lunch. dinner. first come, first served

north kansas city / inner kansas city (ks) >

K: First thing to note. If you absolutely must have *Stroud's* famous pan-fried chicken on a Friday night, then have a snack before you go because a good portion of this town is also dreaming of *Stroud's* famous pan-fried chicken. Second thing to note. Though the chicken is fried perfection, what I will dream of until I'm withered are the *Stroud's* cinnamon rolls. I was so besotted with these gooey divine caloric wonders that I ate mine and then realized I forgot to take pictures. Silly, greedy me. I hoped that Jon had taken a picture, but alas the cinnamon rolls rendered him useless also.

imbibe / devour:
ice tea
homemade chicken noodle soup
family style pan-fried chicken dinner
pan-fried pork chops
fried livers & gizzards
chicken pot pie tuesdays!
chicken tettrazini fridays!
the cinnamon rolls!!!!!

succotash

brunchonette
15 east third street. in the river market
816.421.2807
tue - sun 9a - 3p wed dinner 6 - 9p

opened in 2001. owner: beth barden
$ - $$: all major credit cards accepted
breakfast. lunch. dinner. first come, first served

river market >

J: There are many reasons I could tell you to go to *Succotash*, but there's a clincher that keeps me coming back. See if you can guess what it is from this list: Every inch of the enormous pear pecan pancake is delicious. The weekly three-course dinner menu is the best deal in town. Coffee comes in random thrift store mugs and if you go often enough you might get a Batman one. The environment is funky and perfect to hang out in and run into your friends. The rainbow layer cake is loopily breathtaking. Can't guess what's the clincher? I'm not going to tell.

imbibe / devour:
with love from jack lalanne juices
pear pecan pancakes
burrito of love
warm brie & figs
chopped cobb salad
old school tuna melt
yes, it's a real cake cake

taqueria camecuaro

authentic homestyle mexican food
309 north seventh street. between splitlog and ohio
913.281.4363
mon - sun 8a- 9p

opened in 2002. owner: fernando tapia
$: cash
lunch. dinner. first come, first served

north kansas city > **e41**

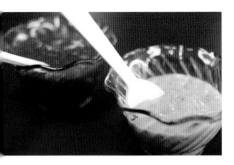

J: You know every city with a decent sized Hispanic community has to have one—it is just a matter of finding it. I'm talking about an authentic taco and burrito place that has killer food. Kaie and I knew that a place like this had to exist in KC, so we did a little digging and came up with *Taqueria Camecuaro* which is known more for the connecting carniceria and tortilleria. This is the real deal, but note: there's no printed menu, not much atmosphere and not much English spoken. If you can get beyond these hurdles and do some gesturing like we did, you will hit the deliciousness jackpot.

imbibe / devour:
horchata
fresh flour tortillas made on site
tacos
tortas
burritos:
  carnitas
  al pastor
  tinga

the better cheddar

cheese and gourmet delicacies

ccp: 604 west 48th street. between pennsylvania and jefferson
pv: prairie village shopping center, number five. between 71st and mission
ccp: 816.561.8204 / pv: 913.362.7575 www.thebettercheddar.com
see website for hours

opened in 1983. owner: ron shalinsky
$$: all major credit cards accepted
grocery. first come, first served

country club plaza / prairie village > e42

K: In my early years I was pretty ho-hum about cheese. It was something that was best in a jar—Cheez Whiz and I were on close terms. Then I moved to NYC and French triple creams caught my fancy. By the time I met my future husband who sells cheese for a living, I had developed a big fat cheese crush. Though these days you can find decent cheeses at the big grocery stores, the ultimate place to buy the really good stuff is *The Better Cheddar*. Here the staff knows their cheeses, whether they be goat, sheep or cow's. And there's a swell selection of gourmet foodstuffs to supplement with. It's all good.

imbibe / devour:
tealicious teas
moxie original elixir
villa manodori aceto balsamico
quicke's english farmhouse cheddar
drunken goat
cypress grove farms lambchopper
gina & sofia barley flour tagliatelle
assorted european candies

the filling station

coffee, sandwiches, salads, juices and happiness

2980 mcgee traffic way. between gillham and cherry
816.931.4335 www.fillingstationcoffee.com
mon - sun 6:30a - 6p

opened in 2004. owner: robin krause
$ - $$: all major credit cards accepted
breakfast. lunch. coffee / tea. first come, first served

union hill > **e43**

J: *The Filling Station* is a coffee shop with some obvious parallels to a gas station. For starters, it is housed in a former one. In addition, people come here to be refueled and maintained. This is where the resemblance with a Star Texaco ends as there are no filthy bathrooms, week-old corndogs or cherry hazelnut coffee. *The Filling Station* serves spectacularly good coffee, the food is yummy and the service terrific. Juices, such as the liquid sunshine, are so fresh and bright you will surely glow after ingestion. This is the perfect place for a tune-up.

imbibe / devour:
the liquid sunshine
broadway coffee drinks
yo granny smoothie
cucumber mint salad
artichoke & black olive salad
the slammer
tuna melt
fresh cookies

the peanut

famous for the wings

5000 main street. corner of 50th
816.753.9499
brunch sun 10a - noon grill mon - sat 11a - midnight sun 10a - 11p
(google to find the three other locations)

opened in 1933. owner: melinda kenny
$: mc. visa
lunch. dinner. brunch. first come, first served

country club plaza >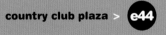

J: Through trusted sources, I was informed the wings at *The Peanut* were a Kansas City must but that I might not like the environment. So I went to the original Peanut and tried the famous wings. I concurred they were peppery perfection. But my informant got the environment part wrong. I loved the jumbled décor filled with dusty KC memorabilia. Sure, it's a dive, but it's the very best kind—it's a dive turned institution. This is where KCers go after a game, meet friends, watch sports or just grab a pint. You'll find all ages, all income levels. It's a hodgepodge, and a good one at that.

imbibe / devour:
beer
mixed drinks
the buffalo chicken wings
triple blt
reuben
hot dawg
chili cheese fries
spicy eggs for brunch

the upper crust

homemade pies and more

115 westport road (inside prydes). corner of 40th
816.561.4990 www.prydeskitchen.com
fri - sat 10a - 6p

opened in 2005. owners: jan knobel and elaine van burkirk
$ - $$: mc. visa
treats. first come, first served

westport >

J: As you'll read in the shop section of this book, I heart *Pryde's Olde Westport* kitchenware shop. One of the reasons I feel the love for it is the bakery that's tucked away on the lower floor, *The Upper Crust*. All the pies that Jan and Elaine make are made from scratch with buttery crusts and fillings like crimson appleberry, rhubarb and banana cream. Yes, they are just like your grandmother used to make if she was Betty Crocker. This place almost seems too good to be true—a culinary superstore *and* a pie bakery. Have I died and gone to foodie heaven?

imbibe / devour:
pies:
  lemon meringue
  sour cream raisin
  german chocolate
  gooseberry
  bumbleberry
quiche of the day
burnt sugar frosted banana cookies

town topic

old-fashioned hamburgers and quality breakfasts

2021 broadway street. corner of 20th
1900 baltimore avenue. corner of 19th
broadway: 816.842.2298 / baltimore: 816.471.6038
broadway: 24/7 baltimore: mon - fri 5:30a - 2:30p sat 6:30a - 1:30p

opened in 1937. owner: scott sparks
$: all major credit cards accepted
breakfast. lunch. dinner. first come, first served

crossroads arts district > **e46**

K: B-a-r-g-a-i-n-s are important these days, even if you've got money in the bank. Sure you could go do the fast food thing and then pay loads of money after the fact talking to a shrink about fast food guilt. Or you could head to *Town Topic* for a burger which has been delicious since 1937 and will only set you back $2.05. I suggest you invest just a bit more and have one of *TT's* thick and delicious shakes. Want to throw caution to the wind and eat like it's 2007? Order a piece of pie. Though they don't make them from scratch, they do have a whole slew to choose from. Go ahead, live a little.

imbibe / devour:
root beer float
hand-dipped shakes
hot cakes
truck stop omelet
bigger burger with cheese
coney dog
grilled cheese & tots
lotsa pies

velvet creme popcorn

flavored popcorn and more

4710 belinder road. corner of 47th
913.236.7742 www.velvetcremepopcorn.com
mon - sat 9a - 5:30p

opened in 1937. owner: nance white-wright
$: all major credit cards accepted
treats. first come, first served

inner kansas city (ks) >

J: Did you know that we can thank the Aztecs for popcorn? In 1519 Cortes caught his first sight of the fluffy stuff as he invaded Mexico and saw the Aztecs using it as decoration for ceremonial headdresses and necklaces. Do you think Cortes knew those necklaces were potentially delicious? And thank you *Velvet Creme* for taking popped corn to new heights by covering it with delicious flavours like caramel, cinnamon and cheese and putting it in large decorated tins, then mailing it all over the world. The world is a better place because of the Aztecs and *Velvet Creme*.

imbibe / devour:
popcorn flavors:
  buttered
  cheese
  caramel
  cinnamon
  sour cream & onion
  chili cheese
  white chocolate almond

yj's snack bar

coffee, food and friends

128 west 18th street. between wyandotte and baltimore
816.472.5533 myspace.com/yjs_snack_bar
mon - wed 7:30a - 10p thu - sat 24/7 sun til midnight

opened in 1928. owner: david ford
$: mc. visa
lunch. dinner. first come, first served

crossroads arts district > e48

J: Here's the thing with *YJ's*—you either get it or you don't. At first glance, it seems eensy weensy and seriously funky. The two wobbly outside tables are occupied by smoking hipsters. If you are pulling up with three kids in a Dodge Caravan, this place might not be your cup of tea. If you're a wordpress guru riding by on your '78 Schwinn Stingray, you'll love *YJ's*. The coffee's good, the food plentiful and cheap with nightly specials, and there's dj's on occasion. There are a load of people in this town that not only seem to get *YJ's*, they worship at its funky altar.

imbibe / devour:
house coffee
breakfast sandwich
specials:
  soul food
  mexican tostadas
  north african
  feta feast
  fish fry & red beans

you say tomato

homegrown goodness served daily
2801 holmes street. corner of 28th
816.756.5097 www.ystkc.com
tue - sat 7a - 3p sun 9a - 2p

opened in 2006. owners: michael pouncil, randy parks and mark wingard
$ - $$: mc. visa
breakfast. lunch. grocery. first come, first served

dutch hill >

K: I could do a riff here on "you say tomato, I say tamato," but that's just too lazy. Instead I will pontificate on one of my favorite things: pie for breakfast. When Jon and I entered *You Say Tomato* we gave each other "the look." Specifically the "I really like this place, so you better like this place" look. We explored the little grocery section, but then I eyed the pies at the counter where orders are made for the café part of *YST*, and I could think of nothing else. I think Jon had to stop me from doing my little pie for breakfast jig because I was so happy. Jon reports everything else here is good also since I was indisposed of.

imbibe / devour:
harney & sons teas
lost trail sodas
asparagus, red pepper & goat cheese quiche
the classic blt
ground beef bierocks
jane's famous knish
rice crispy treats
fresh blackberry pie

about

• All of the businesses featured in this book are locally owned. In deciding which businesses to feature, we require this criteria first and foremost. Then we look for businesses that strike us as utterly authentic, whether they be new or old, chic or funky. We are not an advertorial guide, therefore businesses do not pay to be featured.

• The maps in this guide are not highly detailed but instead are representational of each area noted. We highly suggest, if you are visiting, to also have a more detailed map. Streetwise Maps are always a good bet, and are easy to fold up and take along with you. Explore from neighborhood to neighborhood. Note that almost every neighborhood featured has dozens of great stores and restaurants other than our favorites listed in this book. We also have a Google map of KC with the indicators of the businesses noted at http://tiny.cc/5ruSG . Paste this into the browser of your phone, it's quite useful.

• Make sure to double check the hours of the business before you go by calling or visiting its website. Often the businesses change their hours seasonally. The pictures and descriptions of each business are representational—please don't be distraught when the business no longer carries or is not serving something you saw or read about in the guide.

• Small local businesses have always had to work that much harder to keep their heads above water. During this economic downturn, many will close. We apologize if some of the businesses featured here are no longer open.

• The eat.Shop clan consists of a small crew of creative types who travel extensively and have dedicated themselves to great eating and interesting shopping around the world. Each of these people writes, photographs and researches his or her own books, and though they sometimes do not live in the city of the book they author, they draw from a vast network of local sources to deepen the well of information used to create the guides.

• Please support the local bookstores in KC. There's a couple featured in this book, to find the others, go to: http://www.Indiebound.org/indie-store-finder

• There are three ranges of prices noted for restaurants, $ = cheap, $$ = medium, $$$ = expensive

eat.shop.sleep

here are many great places to stay in kc, but here are a few of our picks:

the q hotel & spa
560 westport road (westport)
816.931.0001 / theqhotel.com
standard double from $100
notes: the first green hotel in kc with complimentary continental breakfast

hotel phillips
106 west 12th street (downtown)
816.221.7000 / hotelphillips.com
standard double from $150
restaurant: 12 baltimore
notes: stylish boutique hotel centrally located

the raphael hotel
325 ward parkway (country club plaza)
800.821.5343 / raphaelkc.com
standard double from $170
restaurant: chaz on the plaza
notes: elegant, european style boutique hotel

southmoreland on the plaza b&b
116 east 46th street (country club plaza)
816.531.7979 / southmoreland.com
standard double from $130
notes: a luxurious b&b with jacuzzis in the room and gourmet breakfast

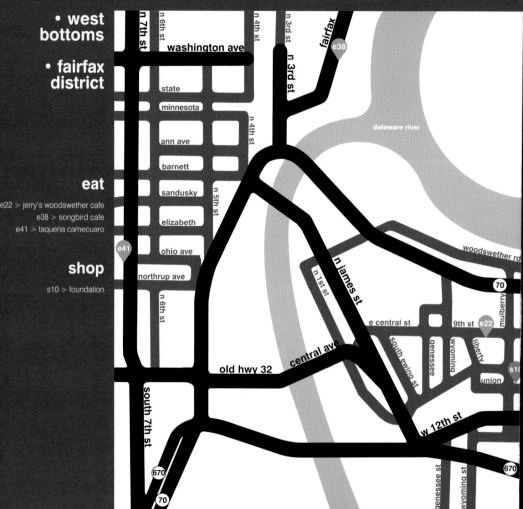

- **west bottoms**
- **fairfax district**

eat

e22 > jerry's woodswether cafe
e38 > songbird cafe
e41 > taqueria camecuaro

shop

s10 > foundation

washington ave

state
minnesota
ann ave
barnett
sandusky
elizabeth
ohio ave
northrup ave

n 7th st
n 6th st
n 4th st
n 3rd st
fairfax
n 3rd st
n 4th st
n 5th st
n 6th st

e38

deleware river

woodswether rd

70

n james st
n 1st st

e central st
9th st
e22
mulberry
liberty
s10
union

central ave
south ewing st
genessee
wyoming

old hwy 32

south 7th st

w 12th st

670
70

genessee st
wyoming st
670

note. all maps face north

river market •
columbus •
park

eat

e3 > baby cakes
e9 > cascone's grill
e19 > habashi mart
e20 > happy gillis
e25 > le fou frog
e40 > succotash

shop

s18 > hung-vuong market
s24 > polivka
s29 > river market antique mall
s34 > the planters seed &
spice company

note: all maps face north

• downtown

eat

e37 > savoy grill

shop

s15 > harry j epstein co

note: all maps face north

crossroads • arts district

westside •

westside • north

eat

e1 > 1924 main
e6 > bluebird bistro
e10 > cellar rat
e11 > christopher elbow
e12 > city tavern
e16 > fervere bakery
e18 > grinders
e26 > lill's on 17th
e29 > michael smith
e32 > paleterias tropicana
e33 > pizza bella
e46 > town topic
e48 > yj's

shop

s2 > acme bicycle company
s3 > antiquities and oddities
architectural salvage
s4 > birdies
s5 > black bamboo
s11 > gallup map company
s14 > hammerpress
s17 > hudson home
s23 > peggy noland
s28 > retro inferno
s30 > spool
s32 > the darling room
s33 > the orchid loft

note: all maps face north

- **hospital hill**
  - **union hill**
  - **dutch hill**

eat

e43 > the filling station
e49 > you say tomato

shop

s21 > museo

note: all maps face north

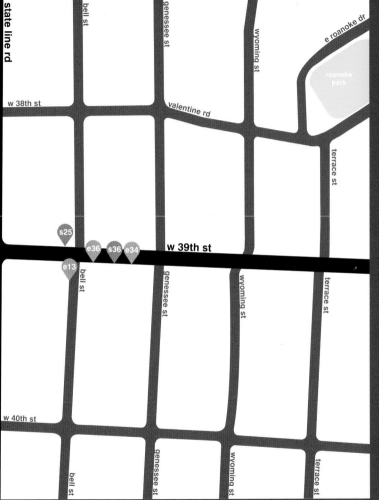

39th •

eat

e13 > d'bronx
e34 > po's dumpling bar
e36 > room 39

shop

s25 > prospero's books
s36 > volker bikes

note: all maps face north

• westport

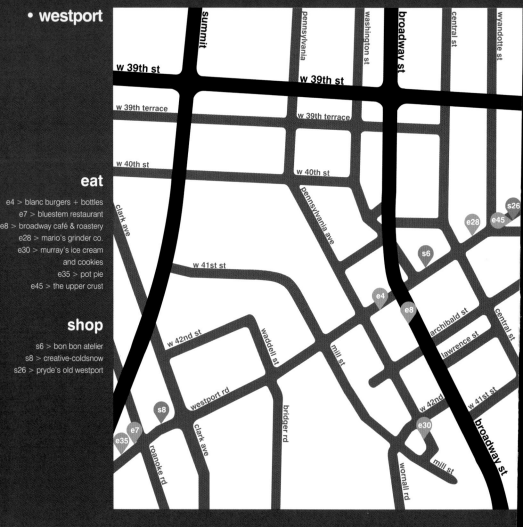

eat

e4 > blanc burgers + bottles
e7 > bluestem restaurant
e8 > broadway café & roastery
e28 > mario's grinder co.
e30 > murray's ice cream
and cookies
e35 > pot pie
e45 > the upper crust

shop

s6 > bon bon atelier
s8 > creative-coldsnow
s26 > pryde's old westport

note: all maps face nor

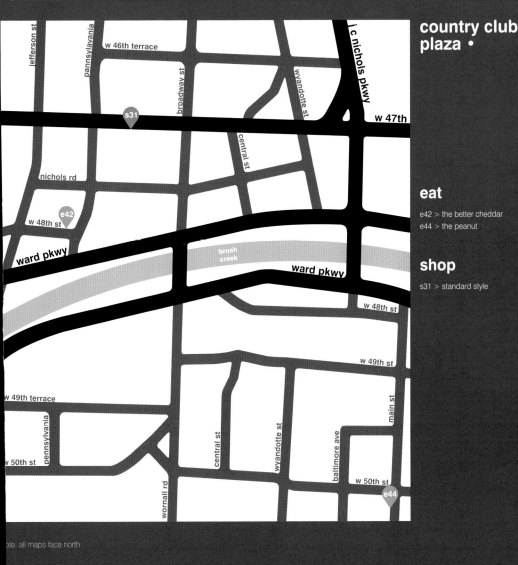

country club
plaza •

eat

e42 > the better cheddar
e44 > the peanut

shop

s31 > standard style

note: all maps face north

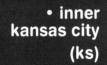

• inner
kansas city
(ks)

eat

e21 > hi hat coffee
e31 > oklahoma joe's barbeque
e39 > strouds
e47 > velvet creme popcorn

shop

s1 > 45th & state line arts and
antiques district
s19 > matney floral design

note: all maps face nor

brookside •
crestwood •

eat

e5 > blue grotto
e24 > la cucina di mamma

shop

s7 > brookside toy & science
s12 > george
s27 > reading reptile

note: all maps face north

• prairie village

eat

e14 > dolce baking
e42 > the better cheddar

shop

s9 > curious sofa
s16 > haught style

granada ln
granada rd
fontana st
el monte st
w 67th terrace
delmar ln
w 68th terrace
w 69th st
69th
prairie ln
oxford
s16
e42
s9
w 89th terrace
69th
e14
w 70th st
w 70th terrace
granada
w 71st
w 71st terrace
w 72nd
w 72nd terrace
alhambra st
village dr
w 72nd terrace
w 73rd st
w 73rd terrace
w 74th st
w 74th terrace
w 74th
fontana st
el monte
w 73rd terrace
w 74th st

mission rd
mission rd
cherokee ln
tomahawk rd
w 68th st
w 69th st

indian hills
country club

w 71st
cherokee dr
canterbury
windsor
park
falmouth st

note: all maps face nor[t]

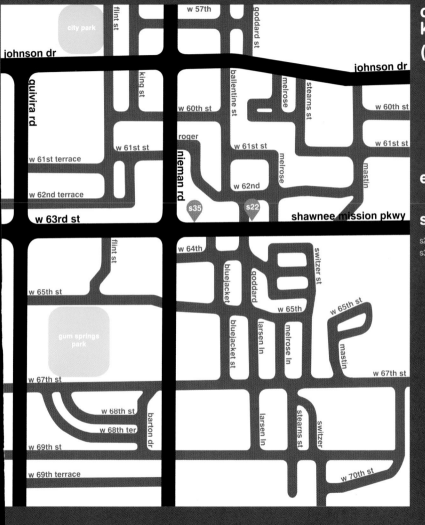

outer •
kansas city
(ks)

eat

shop

s22 > nigro's western store
s35 > vinyl renaissance

note: all maps face north

- **leawood**
- **martin city**

eat

e23 > jess and jim's steak house

shop

s13 > habitat
s20 > mitzy london's

note: all maps face nor

45th & state line
arts and antique district

a whole street of antique stores

west 45th street. corner of state line road
hours vary at each location

owners vary. see a list of businesses
on the next page

inner kansas city (ks) > **s01**

K: I spent quite a bit of time in Kansas City driving up and down State Line Road. I like this road. The neighborhoods around it are beautiful and sometimes stately, and there's the thrill that if you turn one way you're in Kansas, the other in Missouri. One night as I was driving back toward town, I caught a glimpse of a street lined with glowing lanterns. Illegal u-turn ensued. Within minutes I was walking along the row of antique stores on 45th. It was a festive night—everybody was browsing the glorious wares at the different establishments, sipping champagne. There's magic to be found here.

covet:
45th street businesses:
  christopher filley
  parrin & co.
  kincaids
  earl's court
  show-me antiques
  portabello road
  morning glory

acme bicycle company

killer bikes and custom work

412 east 18th street. between oak and locust
816.221.2045 www.acmebicyclecompany.com
tue - wed 11a - 6p thu noon - 7p fri 11a - 6p sat 11a - 3p

opened in 2004. owners: christi lynne and sarah gibson
mc. visa

crossroads arts district > **s02**

J: The bike world is a tight-knit group. I am talking about serious bikers, people whose bicycles are their sole transportation rain or shine, not those who scoot around on their Huffy on the most perfect day in July. As a result, bike-o-philes and the bike stores they shop at can seem cripplingly intimidating—something *Acme Bicycle Co.* is not. It is the only custom frame shop in Kansas City offering new, used and custom gear. *Acme* will not only help you find a perfect ride for your workday commute, but for those inclined they will make a custom tall bike, the perfect accessory as ringleader of your new bike posse.

covet:
masi
se
red line
surly
origin
breezer
brook saddles
deller hats

antiquities & oddities
architectural salvage

a warehouse of antiques and more

2045 broadway street. corner of southwest
816.283.3740 www.aoarchitecturalsalvage.com
thu - sat 10a - 5p

opened in 1998. owner: rick bettinger
mc. visa

crossroads arts district > **s03**

K: If you did architectural salvage at my house you wouldn't find much more than disingtegrating old stucco and fossilized dog dung. So don't come to my house. Instead, head to *Antiques & Oddities*. Here you will find what amounts to a city full of relics. This is not a place to dash into quickly. You must dedicate some real time to dig in and explore as there are nooks and crannies aplenty. If I could have taken home anything, it would have been the massive wood doors that once were part of a bank. Alas, they live permenantly at *A&O*. I'll have to find something a little more my size.

covet:
art deco wall sconces
'60s charles eames style retro light fixture
stained glass
doors of all shapes & sizes
old advertising signs
crane vitreous china sink
antique bicycles
marble mantles

birdies

lovely lingerie

116-118 west 18th. between baltimore and wyandotte
816.842.2473 www.birdiespanties.com
tue - sat noon - 7p

opened in 2003. owners: peregrine honig jr. partner: danielle meister
mc. visa

crossroads arts district > **s04**

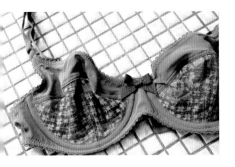

K: Ladies, I have a question for you. Do you wear pretty lingerie every day? If you do, I want to be like you. If you don't, you are like me—lingerie lazy. When there are places like *Birdies* around, there is no excuse for wearing anything other than scrumptious underthings. Even though *Birdies* occupies a teensy space, there are heeps to choose from here, and you are guaranteed a helpful hand to find what tickles your fancy whether it be a spectacular bra-and-panty set or just a simple pair of undies. *Birdies* is here on this earth to remind me and the ladies of KC that pretty lingerie is essential.

covet:
marlies dekkers
the little bra company
huit
clo
arianne
mary greene
stella replied
birdies bath salts

black bamboo

asian antiques and modern furnishings
1815 wyandotte street. between 18th and 19th
816.283.3000 www.black-bamboo.com
tue - fri 10a - 6p sat 10a - 5p

opened in 2004. owner: tim butt
all major credit cards accepted
design services

crossroads arts district > s05

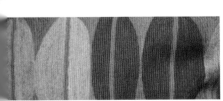

J: There are numerous home design trends I have regrettably embraced, like faux granite furniture and torchiere lamps. Unlike me, the refined Asian cultures have been cultivating good taste for thousands of years seemingly without the unfortunate missteps. The home design store *Black Bamboo* embraces this refined aesthetic. Their store is an eclectic mix of Asian antiques presented in a modern vernacular. An antique Burmese lacquer box looks entirely modern when presented on a contemporary Wonder Works table. I'm a convert—no more marshmallow comfort easy chairs in my home.

covet:
selenite multi tea light log
felt rocks
porcelain cherry blossoms
middle kingdom porcelain
margo selby pillows
burmese betel boxes
aviva stanoff pillows
wonder works

bon bon atelier

a delectable boutique

314 westport road. between broadway and central
816.756.0855 www.bonbonatelier.com
mon - sat 10a - 6p

opened in 2006. owners: betsy blodgett and emily blodgett-panos
mc. visa
online shopping

westport > 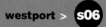 s06

J: At *eat.shop* we feature people who are doing what might be the second oldest profession in the world. I'm talking about creating something and selling it themselves. From wizened Mexican women hand-molding tortillas to eccentric French men designing couture dresses, there is something fundamental about creative people selling their own wares. The sisters at *Bon Bon Atelier* are doing just this. In their adorable, candybox-like shop, they sell their designs along with items from other creatives that make you look cute and sassy and not at all like you are practicing the oldest profession in the world.

covet:
bon bon atelier clothing
emetalworks.com
dirty laundry
shinzi katoh cards
fashion illustrators by laird borelli
pink studio
david aubrey cuff
mor cosmetics

brookside toy & science

from toys to taxidermy

330 west 63rd street. between brookside and wornall
816.523.4501 www.brooksidetoyandscience.com
mon - fri 10a - 6p sat 10a - 5p sun noon - 4p

opened in 1964. owners: jim and mary jo ward
all major credit cards accepted
online shopping

brookside >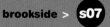

SHARK   SHARK

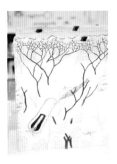

J: *Brookside Toy and Science* feels like a toy store that is owned by a mad scientist. Timeless classics like Legos and Lincoln Logs are sold alongside not-so-classics like sharks in formaldehyde and taxidermied aardvarks frozen into cute poses. German-made Haba Toys are for sale next to a small purse made from a preserved frog. This fanciful mix might mystify the adult set, but kids will go positively gaga over the diverse offerings. Adults, just think of some of the more unusual offerings as nature's toys—and remember back to when you collected dried worms and rocks.

covet:
britains toys
rody horse
fossils & minerals
elenco snap rover
sharks in jars
sparkle the duckling
chemistry kits
plan toys

creative-coldsnow

artist materials

808 - 814 westport road. between roanoke and clark
816.531.1213 www.creativecoldsnow.com
(see website for second location)
mon - fri 9a - 7p sat 9a - 5p sun noon - 5p

opened in 1980. owners: bill and marianne mckean
all major credit cards accepted
online shopping

westport >

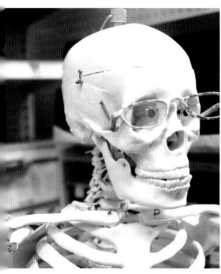

J: There is nothing more satisfying than creating something brand new, 100% from scratch. This applies to all kinds of creating: food, music, buildings, babies and artwork—just to name a few. In the artwork category, the place to get started is *Creative-Coldsnow*. This art supply has a range of materials that is truly comprehensive, from high-end drafting equipment to oil paints to scale model skeletons to baking soda rockets. If you can dream it, you can make it with the range of items here. As far as making babies, you are on your own with that one.

covet:
sennelier paints
the meteor baking soda & vinegar rocket
scale model skeleton
essex brushes
random heads
daler-rowney sketchpads
hobein paints
mini field plus paint kits

HEADS
YOUR CHOICE

curious sofa

an array of home furnishings, accessories and unusual items

3925 west 69th terrace. in the prairie village shops
913.432.8969 www.curioussofa.com
mon - sat 10a - 6p sun noon - 5p

opened in 2000. owner: debbie dusenberry
all major credit cards accepted

prairie village > **s09**

K: My mother has the touch when it comes to decorating her house for a holiday. Whether it be Easter or Halloween, Fourth of July or Christmas—her home magically becomes transformed. I loved it as a child and still love it as an adult. The moment I walked into *Curious Sofa,* I wished my mom was with me. We would have ahhhed in unison at the snowy scene. Everything was shades of silver, cream and white—even the most hardened grinch of a shopper would melt at the sight. Debbie reminds us with her magical store that shopping is an experience, not a chore.

covet:
sofas, of course
antique bronze bed
costume pearls
bella notte bedding
jeanette farrier scarf
vintage photos & pretty papers
pickwick + co. candles
seasonal delights

135

foundation

architectural reclamation
1221 union avenue. corner of mulberry
816.283.8990 www.foundationkc.com
tue - sat 11a - 5p

opened in 2006. owner: patrick ottesen
mc. visa
architectural re-use services. event space

west bottoms > **s10**

K: I love architectural salvage places. To me they are like time capsules that you get to explore in the present day. Wandering around *Foundation* felt like getting a snapshot into KC's past, from the old *Town Topic* signage to the massive six-arm lights that came from a local church. Though I knew I had no use for either of these objects, I eyed literally half a dozen other things that I did have use for. Then Jon came up and pointed out to me a big old chopping block he lusted for. Before we knew it, we were making plans to rent a U-Haul. This is the effect *Foundation* will have on you.

covet:
modern six-arm hanging light
town topic street sign
knoll multi-seat bench
maple butcher block
gothic oak altar rail
leonard seabring self portrait
double basin lab sink
reclaimed architectural elements

137

gallup map company

for ultimate maps and more

1733 main street. between 17th and 18th
816.842.1994 www.gallupmaps.com
mon - fri 9a - 5p

opened in 1969. owner: patricia carroll
all major credit cards accepted
online shopping

crossroads arts district > **s11**

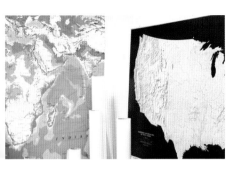

J: I'm worried about the future of maps. They already had a bad rap because no one can fold them up correctly. Then iPhones and Garmins came along, and the map is suddenly an endagered species. I think maps should be considered works of art. It's fascinating to see a city or state meticulously reproduced in colorful squiggles and blocks of color. *Gallup Maps* has been around since 1875 so they understand that a map can be utilitarian as well as artful. Now if they could just get maps to play music, they could give Apple a run for their money.

covet:
3-d map of missouri
mark-it dots
wall map mural
globes
lake of the ozarks survey map
map of iran
aerial mural of kansas city
american flags

george

a lifestyle store
315 east 55th street. between brookside and oak
816.361.2128 www.georgelifestyle.com
mon - sat 10a - 5p

opened in 2002. owner: george terbovich
visa. mc

crestwood >

K: Sometimes it takes a bit of time for me to think about what I'm going to write about a business. I'm not having this issue with *George* because it all boils down to one simple statement: *George* is stunning. Rarely do I enter a retail environment that stops me in my tracks. What strikes me the most here is the simplicity of the story: beautiful objects ranging from furniture to totes, from vintage to handcrafted, from pricey to affordable. Each piece here is arranged in a way that allows it to shine—there's no clutter, no fuss. And for me, there's no problem loving every square inch of *George*.

covet:
pair of regency chairs
1880 french drying rack
cashmere throws & scarves
painted cast-iron cowheads
beautifully chosen art books
handmade leather bags
home floor cushions
select assortment of bath products

habitat

the best shoe store in kansas city
4569 west 119th street. at one nineteen shops
913.451.6360 www.habitatshoes.com
mon - sat 10a - 9p sun noon - 6p

opened in 2005. owners: john and kristen mcclain
visa. mc
online shopping

leawood > **s13**

K: On the day that I visited *Habitat*, I was feeling run down. As I was taking pictures of shoe after fantastic shoe, I whined away with John patiently listening. After I finished, it slipped out that the night before was a big event at the store and during the event John was called away to take one of his children to the hospital after busting his chin open, and that his third child had been born just three days earlier. Holy shoeshine—the McClains can obviously do it all, and at the top of the list is having the sharpest shoe store (plus women's and men's clothing and accessories) in KC. They are my heroes.

covet:
shoes:
  loeffler randall
  chie mahara
  j shoes
clothing & accessories:
  mae
  freitag
  spiewak

hammerpress

letterpress and design studio

110 southwest boulevard. between wyandotte and baltimore
816.421.1929 www.hammerpress.net
tue - fri 10a - 5:30p sat noon - 5p

opened in 1994. owner: brady vest
all major credit cards accepted
online shopping

crossroads arts district >

J: Artists interested in the tactile and mechanical art of letterpress are a specific kind of artist. They must employ both sides of their brain, being driven by aesthetics as well as the mechanics of how something is made. *Hammerpress's* Brady is such a person. His damn fine taste is in perfect balance with the subtle and industrial art of letterpress. At this studio / retail showroom, take your time to take it all in, from the rock posters to greeting cards to custom designed wedding invites. Somehow Brady makes this craft from a bygone era feel totally modern and new.

covet:
hat series postcards
extra good tidings cards
santa crest mini art print
happy winter boxed notes
hammerpress t's
my morning jacket poster
amore gift enclosure cards
custom design work

harry j. epstein co.

tools, hardware and discoveries

301 west eighth street. corner of central
816.421.4752 www.harryepstein.com
mon - fri 8a - 4:30p sat 8:30a - noon

opened in 1930. owners: steve and ken sackin
mc. visa

downtown >

J: I found an East German bomb shelter light circa 1960 still in the box at *Harry J. Epstein's*—try to buy that at Home Depot. Even if you're not a total gearhead, you will find this family-run business a cool place. Along with your standard screwdrivers and hammers, you'll find anything from wrenches for giants (or for building bridges) to tin flasks from the former Soviet Union. This is the kind of place where you stop to get a few screws for a home improvement project and leave with a cartographer's desk from Finland because it was too awesome to pass up. *Epstein's* is a treasure.

covet:
m.s.a. hat
bahco saws
grommet kits
super magnets
dexter russel knives
dixie draw shave
klein tool bag
gerber backpack axe

haught style

stylish togs

6951 tomahawk road. in prairie village shopping center
913.677.0070 www.haughtstyle.com
mon - fri 10a - 7p sat 10a - 6p sun 1 - 5p

opened in 2007. owner: laura haught oxandale
all major credit cards accepted

prairie village > **s16**

K: When I walked into this store I, couldn't get that song by David Johansen out of my mind—"Hot Hot Hot." It just kept looping around on my internal iPod, and it was interfering with my exploration of *Haught Style*. Finally I was able to silence this bothersome soundtrack and get down to business, and I could see that there was plenty to swoon for—or even be "hot" for (sorry, now I can't stop myself). Laura has a good eye for what the ladies of Kansas City want to wear, and the day I was there the place was bustling with activity. That's hot.

covet:
sharon segal
by francine
emma & posh
twelfth street by cynthia vincent
kooba bags
max & cleo
pink dove jewelry
phillip bloch

hudson home

modern furnishings

1500 grand boulevard, second floor. corner of 15th
816.421.3629 www.hudsonhomeonline.com
mon - sat 11a - 5:30p

owners: bill poole and sofia varanka
all major credit cards accepted
custom orders / design

crossroads arts district > **s17**

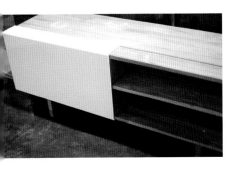

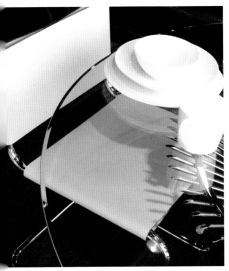

K: During these days of economic uncertainty, are you tempted to buy all of your home furnishings at budget outlets? I know it makes sense for the bank account, but let me counter with the idea of visiting *Hudson Home*. Here you will find pieces by some of the finest small manufacturers of home furnishings in the U.S., like Blu Dot. Their pieces are clean, modern and well built. As for affordability, aren't you willing to pay more for something that will last? I say, yay for good design and craftsmanship, and nay for the cheap stuff that you know will be in the dump in a year.

covet:
blu dot anything
mash studios lax series
mortise & lenon carter drum tables
amenity organic bedding
heath ceramics
knoll platner dining table
luzifer mikado suspension
porter teleo hand-painted wall coverings

hung-vuong market

great vietnamese market
303 grand boulevard. corner of fourth
816.221.7754
mon - fri 9:30a - 5:30p sat 8:30a - 7:30p sun 9:30a - 8:30p

all major credit cards accepted

river market >  **s18**

J: The upside to a really good Asian market is that they carry hard-to-find exotic foods like fuyu persimmons. The downside is that stopping in for said persimmons is impossible without leaving with an armful of other goods of the edible and non-edible kind. At a great market like *Hung-Vuong* you are sure to find a number of items that are 100% useful (bamboo cutting boards and porcelain teapots) or completely wacky but irresistable (salted radish candy and large ornate figurines). Either way, shopping here is a heck of a lot more entertaining than at your local Hy-Vee.

covet:
lucky bamboo
steamers
bamboo winnows
cute teapots
asian fruits & veg
gold piggy banks
over-the-top figurines
asian cleavers

THANKS FOR S OPPING AT HUNG-VUO MARKET

matney floral design

gorgeous florals and more
2708 west 53rd street. corner of prospect
913.362.5419
mon - sat 9a - 5p

opened in 1987. owner: chuck matney
all major credit cards accepted
custom orders / design

inner kansas city (ks) > **s19**

K: While Jon and I were driving through the beautiful neighborhoods of Kansas City, we were struck by how gorgeous the landscaping was. Houses and yards in all manner of neighborhoods were carefully kept. Then in perfect synergy with the outside, we would catch glimpses in windows of glorious flower arrangements or lush houseplants. Who could be the talent behind what we were seeing in the windows? One guess would be *Matney Floral Design*. Everything on display here matched up to what we had been seeing all across this town—gorgeous greenery and floral wonder.

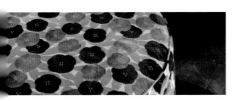

covet:
seda france candles
pineapple vessel
chippendale chairs
magnolia roping
round custom upholstered ottoman
pyrite votives
steward stand wallets
gorgeous custom arrangements

mitzy london's

a vivacious lifestyle and clothing experience
4541 west 119th street. at one nineteen shops
913.661.1775 www.mitzylondons.com
mon - fri 10a - 8p sat 10a - 7p sun 11a - 6p

opened in 2008. owner: mitzy london
all major credit cards accepted

leawood > 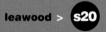 s20

K: The first time I drove by *Mitzy London's* I decided not to go in. I saw the over-the-top window displays and I wimped out. Then a couple days later I was in the 'hood again and decided to rethink my decision. What I found is that *Mitzy London's* is quite extraordinary—it feels like Betsey Johnson and Alexander McQueen's love child of a boutique. There's tartan aplenty mixed up with *Mitzy's* signature hot pink and black—there's everything from clothing to furniture to gifties to even a tea room in the back where high tea is served every Saturday. This place is big fun for grown-up girls.

covet:
mitzy london's line of furniture & clothing
aryn k
active basics
filigree
oh… dear! shoes
moon collection
a guide to quality, taste & style by tim gunn

museo

modern comforts
3021 main street. between 30th and 31st
816.531.3537 www.museousa.com
mon - fri 9a - 5p sat 10a - 4p or by appointment

opened in 1992. owners: darren haun and steve maturo
all major credit cards accepted
custom orders / design services

union hill >  **s21**

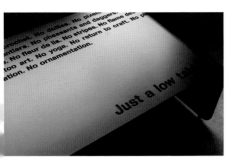

K: Every day while working on this book I would drive up and down Main. And every time I would drive by *Museo*. And every time I would think "that place looks perfect for the book." Finally on the third day I couldn't stand it anymore and headed in to explore *Museo*. I would have been happy not to go much past the first piece I set eyes on, Claud Zellweger's low slung black metal table. Visions of it coming to live at my house danced in my head. Tra la la. Then I came out of my happy trance and explored. This place is all about the best of contemporary design. I wanted it all.

covet:
claude zellweger no ornamentation table
massimo vignelli lines end table
philippe starck caprice chair
magistetti nuvola rossa bookcase
moooi the light shade shade
naota fukasawa bunch 12 vase
poltrona frau palladio sofa

nigro's western store

western stores for the metro cowboy

#1: 3320 merriam lane. between 33rd and 34th
#2: 10509 shawnee mission parkway. between godard and melrose
#1: 913.262.7600 / #2: 913.631.2226 www.nigroswesternstore.com
weekdays 10a - 6p saturdays 10a - 5p

opened in 1972. owners: the nigro family
mc. visa
online shopping

outer kansas city (ks) > **s22**

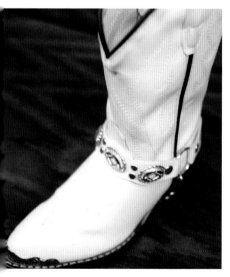

J: I certainly wasn't fooling anyone walking into *Nigro's Western Store*. The nice folks here could tell by looking at me that I would not be buying any tack or a new saddle, yet they welcomed me with a warm howdy as I walked through the door. As I noted, I'm not in the market for the above items and rarely wear cowboy boots, but I have learned there are always gems to be found in a well-stocked western store. A hand-tooled belt or a nice chambray shirt is always in style. *Nigro's* carries all these items, including beautiful Gaier driving gloves that came home with me. Happy me.

covet:
stetson & resistol cowboy hats
boots, boots, boots
minnetonka moccasins
scully shirts
wranglers (of course)
gaier gloves
parkhurst snowy leopard vest
saddles & tack at store #1

peggy noland

totally fun and creative clothing designs
124 west 18th street. between wyandotte and baltimore
816.221.7652 www.peggynoland.com
tue - sat noon - 7p

opened in 2006. owner: peggy noland
all major credit cards accepted
online shopping. custom orders

crossroads arts district > **s23**

J: The day I visited the tiny *Peggy Noland*, its latest incarnation was a sort of fur igloo. Long, synthetic white fur covered the walls and ceiling, and the floor was mirrored. I half expected Snow Miser to appear singing and dancing from behind the fur-covered door. Instead Peggy appeared, and her infectious spirit explained a lot. She is both designer and artist and clearly has a hoot doing what she does. She changes the look of the store to complement her totally original, totally fun clothing designs. Like the Snow Miser, she's too much.

covet:
clothes:
  peggy noland "baby eskimo" line
  peggy noland for "misbehave"
  wini
  piko 1988
  moon collection
  wax
  i. on

polivka

custom woodworking
258 west third street. corner of broadway
816.221.2027 www.dpolivka.com
mon - fri 8a - 5:30p or by appointment

opened in 1993. owner: david polivka
cash only
custom orders / design

river market > **s24**

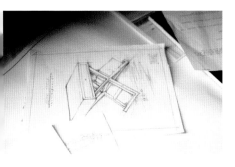

K: At the end of Third Street you'll find yourself under the Broadway Bridge at what seems to be the darkest spot in Kansas City. But if you look hard for the light, you'll find it at the warehouse to your right where *Polivka* is situated. In this big space, David is the mad scientist of woodworking. Jon and I dropped in on him one chilly Saturday afternoon and within moments were deep in conversation about life, about art, about wood! David is a true master of the craft, something even a lay person could see looking at one of his simple, yet intricately crafted dressers. If quality matters, then *Polivka* delivers.

covet:
black walnut dresser
zebra wood bench with wenge top
honduran flame mahogany side chairs
black walnut stools
ebonized mahogany lamp
custom cabinets & casework
wood sculpture

prospero's books

used books and vinyl
1800 west 39th street. corner of bell
816.531.9673 www.prosperosbookstore.com
mon - sat 10:30a - 10p sun 11a - 6p

opened in 1997. owners: tom wayne and will leathem
visa. mc
online shopping

39th >

J: I was first seduced into *Prospero's Books* by the floor-to-ceiling stacks and stacks of used books in what was once a hardware store. Secondarily I was enticed by the depth of offerings—it became quickly clear that this bookstore was where the KC literary community came to roost. Then I took a peek in the basement and found choice selections of used vinyl. Killer stuff like old Hank Williams and rare George Jones records made me start to go a bit crazy. A great selection of used books and awesome vinyl—what more could anybody want? Donuts, maybe?

covet:
a moveable feast by ernest hemingway
the count of monte christo by alexander dumas
slaughterhouse five by kurt vonnegut
hard freeze by philip miller
hart island by melinda hunt
up close & personal live music
the pit
hank williams album

pryde's old westport

a hardware store for cooks

115 westport road. corner of 40th
816.531.5588 www.prydeskitchen.com
mon - sat 10a - 6p

opened in 1968. owner: louise meyers
all major credit cards accepted
online shopping

westport >

J: I have been devoted to a certain cooking store in Paris for a long time. It has been around forever and is chaotically stacked floor to ceiling with all things culinary. I buy something every time I visit. After visiting the KC institution *Pryde's*, I may have to reconsider my devotion. Like my other store, *Pryde's* carries everything, I mean everything culinary. How do they differ? The ladies at *Pryde's* are the nicest, most courteous helpers ever, offering hot coffee and tea as you calmly browse their impressive offerings. Maybe it can be chalked up to cultural differences, but *Pryde's* opened my eyes.

covet:
fiestaware
emile henry cookware
peugeot pepper mills
copper bowls
benedetto cavalieri pasta
lodge cast iron
pequea valley forge hand-forged ironwork
denby dishes

reading reptile

books and tapes for young mammals
328 west 63rd street. between brookside and wornall
816.753.0441 www.readingreptile.com
mon - thu 10a - 6p fri 10a - 6p sat 10a - 5p sun noon - 5p

opened in 1988. owners: debbie pettid and a. bitterman
all major credit cards accepted

brookside >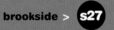

K: I'll eat my kiddo's richly perfumed socks if *Reading Reptile* isn't the coolest children's bookstore to ever grace this planet—even the tagline is cool: "books and tapes for young mammals." Walking in here made me want to throw myself down in only that way somebody under four feet tall can do, grab myself a book and start reading. And it's not just the books and all the cool papier-mâché characters hanging about, it's the book club, the story hours, the groovy art meets book birthday parties. Kids and parents take note: come here soon, come here often—this is what a bookstore should be.

covet:
the wonder book of things to do
we're going on a bear hunt pop-up
the numbers
me and my bike
how to speak dragonese
the nice book
smart feller, fart smeller
free friday films

retro inferno

vintage furnishings from the 20th century

1500 grand boulevard. corner of truman
816.842.4004 www.retroinferno.com
mon - sat 11a - 5:30p

opened in 1998. owner: rod parks
all major credit cards accepted
online shopping

crossroads arts district > **s28**

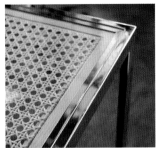

J: Just because something is retro doesn't automatically make it cool. My parents' early american, Susan B. Anthony themed couch could be called 'retro,' and it is not cool. Maybe cool isn't for everyone. But at *Retro Inferno*, the taste of owner Rod is of the refined and modern variety. His large shop is filled with great finds from the mid to late twentieth century. Chairs from Heywood Wakefield and Joe Columbo and tables by Verner Panton and Eileen Gray confirm that *Retro Inferno* has a cultivated vision. Which is a whole lot better than my parents' civil war chic.

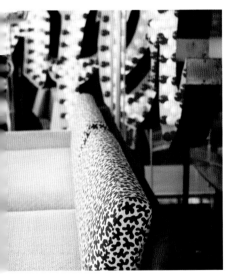

covet:
vermont tubbs snowshoe chairs
chapman brass palm tree lamps
florence knoll walnut top coffee table
george nelson marble top table
milo baughman coggin glass & wicker table
richard schulz chairs
cool memphis stuff
glenn of california storage cabinet

river market antique mall

the friendliest "mall" in town
115 west fifth street. corner of wyandotte
816.221.0220 www.rivermarketantiquemall.com
daily 10a - 6p

opened in 1994. owner: larry mallin
all major credit cards accepted
local delivery

river market >

K: I'm one of those people who thinks I really like antiquing but then when reality strikes gets tired of it after the first store. This is why antique malls are a good thing, and *River Market Antique Mall* is a great thing. I was knee-deep in things I loved within moments of arriving here. When Jon found me, I was juggling my camera and eight Heller plastic mugs. I was ready to leave the camera behind, but Jon convinced me that such a move might be detrimental to this book. So I kept the camera *and* bought the mugs. I'll just need to come back again to get the rest.

covet:
vintage:
  jenfred ware bookends
  career institute instant english handbook
  fur-lined ice skates
  heller dinnerware
  board games
  table hockey
  neon letter

175

spool

a haven for local designers

122 west 18th street. between baltimore and wyandotte
816.842.0228 www.ilovespool.com
tue - sat noon - 7p

opened in 2003. owner: kelly ann allen
mc. visa

crossroads arts district >

K: I find the whole "it" bag phenomenon really strange. Why would you want to have the same bag as everyone else when you could have a one-a-kind-I've-never-seen-anything-like-it-type-of-bag? I found one of these at *Spool* and dubbed it the intestinal bag. The outside looks like a quilted puffer jacket, but then the inside feels like, yes—guts. It's so cool and it's by the extremely talented local designer Ari Fish. Wait, most everything in here is by e.t.l.d.s—many of them grads of Kansas City Art Institute. I think Kelly is the fairy godmother to this diverse group.

covet:
amanda nervig knitted dresses
jennifer boe scarves
bb jeans quilted coat
ari fish intestinal bag
cuties by judy
charitable mittens by alicia
cara long sweet mud clayworks earrings

standard style

stylish but far-from-standard clothing for both sexes

ccp: 447 west 47th street. between pennsylvania and broadway
l: 5076 west 119th street. in the town center plaza
ccp: 913.685.4464 / l: 913.317.8828 www.standardstyle.com
see website for hours

opened in 2003. owners: matt and emily baldwin
all major credit cards accepted
online shopping

country club plaza / leawood > **s31**

J: If only *Standard Style* were the standard by which all people dressed, the world would be a more attractive place. It surely is too much to ask that my high school math teacher, Mrs. Pickles, would have worn the likes of Rock & Republic and Diane Von Furstenburg rather than her shapeless elastic-waist pants and bone-colored twin set. But it is fun to dream. In the meantime, Matt and Emily can supply us with the young, stylish silhouettes that are sexy and sought after. And maybe, just maybe, that will begin to raise the bar for a more attractive world.

covet:
current / elliot
joe's jeans
alexander wang
3.1 philip lim
ksubi
nudie
monrow
elizabeth and james

the darling room

perfect hair-styling products, and oh yes, haircuts

1919 wyandotte. between 19th and sunset
816.474.4647 www.thedarlingroom.com
tue - wed, fri - sat 10a - 6p thu noon - 8p

opened in 2005. owner: amber hodgson
all major credit cards accepted

crossroads arts district > **s32**

K: We don't feature beauty salons in the *eat.shop guides* as they'd have to be re-named the *eat.shop.primp guides*. It doesn't really work for me. But when we came upon *The Darling Room*, it became imperative to make a little exception because this place is soooo gosh-darn cute. I can't talk about Amber's haircuts, though the ladies in the chairs looked quite satisfied. I can talk about the swell product selection she carries that will keep your tresses in the best of condition. My short/curly/frizzy mop was begging me for some Kevin Murphy products. Don't make your hair beg—come in soon.

covet:
products:
  kevin murphy
  bumble + bumble
  lipstick queen
  leonor greyl
  lulu organic hair powder
  marilyn brushes

the orchidloft

orchids and urban gardening

1803 wyandotte street, suite 105. enter on 18th
816.520.2332 www.orchidloft.com
fri - sat 1 - 7p sun by appointment
check website for additional hours

opened in 2008. owner: lindsey meling
mc. visa

crossroads arts district > **s33**

J: Have you ever bought an orchid, enjoyed its exotic beauty for a couple of weeks until the blooms die, and then watched it wither away reminding you that you haven't got what it takes to revive its former glory? You then throw it away... humiliated. Don't be so hasty. You need to head to *The Orchidloft* where Lindsey has created an orchid exchange program. Here's how it works: you buy an orchid, keep it through its peak season, then trade it in when it loses it blooms. You get another that has had the life breathed back into it by Lindsey the orchid-whisperer. Repeat as necessary. Genius.

covet:
phalaenopsis
paphiopedilum
symbidium
dendribium
thymes frasier fir candles
modern pots
blooms in a bag
orchid exchange program

183

the planters seed & spice company

seeds, spices, fertilizers, insecticides and supplies

513 walnut street. between missouri and fifth
816.842.3651 www.plantersseed.com
mon - fri 7a - 6p sat 7a - 5p

opened in 1924
all major credit cards accepted

river market > **s34**

K: My grandfather Red was a grass seed farmer; my other grandfather Otto grew hops. You would think growing things would come naturally to me—but I'm like a deep freeze in June. I kill green things fast. Still, I try to grow things, and *The Planters Seed & Spice Company* is a great place to get materials. There are bushels of seeds here. I'd guess there are enough seeds here to plant a good portion of Kansas. If I come to my senses and decide to not grow (and then destroy) plants, I will still come here for things I can't hurt, like spices or hoses or straw hats.

covet:
seeds, seed & more seeds
bulbs, bulbs & more bulbs
spices
wild bird feed
feed peanuts
heath bird's blend suet cake
wooden bird's houses
dry goods

185

vinyl renaissance

huge selection of collectible vinyl
10922 shawnee mission parkway. corner of nieman
913.962.0014 www.vinyl-renaissance.com
mon - sat 11a - 6p

opened in 2005. owner: dan phillips
mc. visa
online shopping

shawnee > 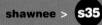 **s35**

J: When I return home from my *eat.shop* research trips, a certain friend always grills me on the truly unique places that were uncovered. She knows that every city will have its chic boutiques and hip bistros. But what this girl is mining for are the places that are funky and undeniably original. When I told her about *Vinyl Renaissance* and its endless rows of collectible classical, opera, rock and jazz vinyl—she flipped out, and I can't print what she actually said, but let's just say she was excited. If you are a record lover, *Vinyl Renaissance* will make you cuss with joy too.

covet:
art tatum *the incomparable*
bill evans *at town hall vol. 1 japan*
the tymes *wonderful wonderful*
1910 fruit gum company *simon says*
jaqueline dupre *saint-saens symphony no. 3*
crabby appleton *rotten to the core*
enrico caruso *sings*
astrud gilberto *look to the rainbow*

volker bikes

rad bikes and accessories

1717 west 39th. between bell and genessee
816.756.5510 www.volkerbicycles.com
mon - fri 11a - 6p sat 10a - 6p sun noon - 5p

opened in 2008. owner: britton kusiak
mc. visa

39th >

J: In my world, bikes have always been cool. As a kid, I begged forever to get a yellow Schwinn with a banana seat and stick shifter. I finally got it and was instantly cool at school. As an adult, I still look at every rad bike that passes by. And maturity has taught me that being cool is more about how you act than what you own. But riding a Swobo del Norte bike from *Volker Bikes* with green rims and tiny handlebars and wearing one of their awesome Portland cycle wear jackets would make me act a certain way, right? And that would be cool.

covet:
swobo del norte bike
pinarello bicycles
brooks saddles
planet bike freddy fenders
colored frogs led lights
portland cycle wear volker jackets
giordana riding jackets
bern helmets

notes

etc.

the eat.shop guides were created by kaie wellman and are published by cabazon books

for more information about the series, or to buy print or online books, please visit: eatshopguides.com

eat.shop kansas city was written, researched and photographed by kaie wellman and jon hart

editing: kaie wellman   copy editing: lynn king   fact checking: emily mattson
map and layout production: julia dickey

kaie + jon thx: all of the great local business owners featured in this book, lard fried fries, brady and lindsay who were the best from day one, the q hotel & spa who made our stay comfortable and convenient, and the robinson family who shared with us their little corner of missouri on a sunny sunday.

cabazon books: eat.shop kansas city
ISBN-13 9780979955785

copyright 2009 © cabazon books

all rights reserved under international and pan-american copyright conventions. no part of this publication may be reproduced, stored in a retrieval system, or transmitted in any form or by any means, electronic, mechanical, photocopying, recording or otherwise, without prior written permission of the copyright owner.

every effort has been made to ensure the accuracy of the information in this book. however, certain details are subject to change. please remember when using the guides that hours alter seasonally and sometimes sadly, businesses close. the publisher cannot accept responsibility for any consequences arising from the use of this book.

the eat.shop guides are distributed by independent publishers group: www.ipgbook.com

PRINTED IN CHINA